7 PRIMARY CHAKRA SYSTEM

An Illustrated Guide to the
7 Primary Chakras

Raven Shamballa
M.S. Counseling, Spiritual Teacher, Pranic Healer, Hypnotherapist

Balboa Press books may be ordered through booksellers or by contacting:

Balboa Press
A Division of Hay House
1663 Liberty Drive
Bloomington, IN 47403
www.balboapress.com
1 (877) 407-4847

ISBN: 978-1-9822-3063-0 (sc)
ISBN: 978-1-9822-3064-7 (e)

Library of Congress Control Number: 2019909016

Print information available on the last page.

Balboa Press rev. date: 01/15/2020

About The Author

In 2014, Raven Shamballa awoke from an operation to find she was a full-blown psychic. After recovered from surgery, she recalled a vision of traveling to the Light Realms and hearing from her Counsel of Masters. She was told by her Counsel of Masters that her psychic gifts would be advanced so she could bring forward a new system of energy healing called Negative Energy Release Work (NERW) and create this book defining the 100 Chakras.

Raven lives in Oceanside, CA, where she works as an energy healer, psychic and psychotherapist. She continues to write books, lead meditation and expand the content of this work online. For more information, see her website - www.ravenlightbody.com, search 'Raven Shamballa' on YouTube, search 'Raven Lightbody' on Facebook, or find 'ravenshamballalightbody' on Instagram.

Readings are available by phone or in person in Oceanside CA, or cities she visits. Psychic readings include past lives, finding your life purpose, angel names, relationship issues, advancing in spiritual practice, psychic development and galactic origins. Negative Energy Release Work is an energy healing technique taught by Raven. For more information on classes and workshops visit her website.

Raven grew up as Monica Kelly in Clovis, CA. Her parents were immigrants. Her mom was born in Rio de Janeiro, Brazil and her father was born in Calcutta, India. After he was converted at a Billy Graham crusade, her father decided to become a Christian minister in America. Raven grew up within a strong Christian faith.

In college, Raven decided to practice hatha yoga to explore her Indian roots. That led to countless workshops on the subject of metaphysics. During this time she lived in a yoga community which introduced her to meditation, Kriya yoga and Raja Yoga. She returned to Fresno for graduate school. She graduated as a Marriage and Family Therapist at California State University Fresno in 2008. After graduation she discovered energy work, spiritual hypnosis and past life regression.

After the psychic opening, a direct connection was established with her angelic team, allowing her to pursue this work of teaching about the energy body and helping others open their psychic gifts.

Other Books by Raven Shamballa

The 100 Chakra Book,
An Introduction to Negative Energy Release Work

This is the foundation teaching material for Raven energy healing practice Negative Energy Release Work (NERW). Raven introduces the concept that humans have 100 chakras, and advanced souls have up to 500 chakras. In the 100 Chakra book, Raven gives a detailed explanation of the 7 Primary Charkas, The Higher Chakras and the Ascending Chakras. She discusses the similarities and differences in the energy body and the soul body, and dives into exoteric concepts of the Higherself, and consciousness. She touches on developing your psychic abilities and working with your angelic team.

NERW has an emphasis on removing negative energies from the energy body, while expanding the soul body in meditation. A self-study, self-healing course is offered in the book to familiarize you with the concepts of the work.

To receive a free energy healing self-study course on the 100 Chakra System, please visit www.ravenlightbody.com

The 3 Pendulum Languages

In this book, Raven explains how you can use the pendulum to start communicating with your white light angelic team. Raven teaches how to contact your angelic team and start communicating with them. Raven's pendulum on the hand language gives a detail explanations of how you can advance your pendulum practice from simple Yes/No/Maybe questions to developing conversations with your team. Raven also explains techniques for working with charts and maps to receive more information.

The 3 Pendulum Languages contains 15 pendulum charts to assist you in conceptualizing a new way to receive information from your angels. Blank charts are provided for you to start your own journey into using this divination tool. Using the pendulum as a tool for angel communication is discusses as a training tool to help develop clairaudience, the ability to hear messages from your angels.

To receive a free download of the Angel Pendulum Chart, go to www.ravenlightbody.com

The 10 Cosmic Dimensions, A Spiritual Guidebook to Ascension

In the book, The 10 Cosmic Dimensions, A Spiritual Guidebook to Ascension, Raven shares information she has received from her guides and the Ascended Masters. She explains the concepts of karma, past lives, life between lives and the Light Realms. The cosmic dimensional scale is a measure of human spiritual evolution. Understanding where you are on the scale and in relationship to other people helps to give insight as to your spirit growth and how to interact with others, especially those lower on the cosmic dimensional scale.

This book includes a self-study course with 10 worksheets to assist you in understanding where you are on the scale.

To receive a free chapter, visit www.ravenlightbody.com

Chakra Balancing with the Pendulum

In the book, Chakra Balancing with the Pendulum, Raven explores the language of the pendulum when working with the 7 Primary Chakras. This book teaches how to read your own chakras and how to balance them. It also gives information on how to read clients' chakras and assist them to balance. Certification courses in Negative Energy Release Work and Chakra Balancing will be taught in the future.

For a free download on chakra balancing, go to www.ravenlightbody.com

For more information on these topics stay connected!

YouTube: Raven Shamballa

Facebook: Raven Lightbody

Instagram: ravenshamballalightbody

Pinterest: ravenlightbody

Introduction to the 7 Primary Chakra Charts

In yoga philosophy, a "chakra" is defined as a spinning whirlpool of energy. There are 7 Primary Chakras located along the spine. These chakras take in negative and positive energy from people and our environment. The 7 Primary Chakras exchange information with our world. Emotions and energies interact with the chakras, which are connected to various psychological and neurological systems in the body.

Energy is exchanged through our daily experience. Therefore, the chakra system is a strong factor in the regulation of mood, emotions, and energy levels. Learning about the chakras, helps you to become aware of which chakras are in-balance or out-of-balance. Through the process of energy clearing and meditation, you'll learn to intentionally open the chakras and release uncomfortable energy. You'll also learn how to balance your energy centers as you move through different situations.

When all the 7 Primary Chakras are open and flowing, one is at optimum. A balanced flow of prana allows you to feel positive energy. You express these positive attitudes in the world and start to fulfill your life's purpose. When there is a current of positive energy flowing through your form, you have activated pranic energy. Pranic energy is defined as positive creative, life-force energy. When you draw pranic flow into your body, you function at your highest self and feel good in your everyday life. The body illuminates with light.

This book provides an illustrated guide and quick reference to the 7 Primary Chakras. Understanding the meaning of the 7 Primary Chakras is important, especially if you are interested in energy healing. This allows you to assess the health of the chakras and identify the blocks in yourself or in others.

As we move through the meanings of the 7 Primary Chakras, the chakra charts serve as a visual learning tool. The visual guide is useful to memorize the names, psychological themes, and positive and negative expressions of each energy center. At the top, three names are given to identify the chakras: the sequential numbers, the English name, and the Sanskrit name.

A few descriptive words are given at the bottom to help memorize the general theme of the chakra. Understanding the general theme of the chakra allows you to pinpoint where there is emotional pain or an energy block.

Chakras 2, 3, 4, 5 & 6 have a front and back. The front of a chakra holds the emotional response to an event or situation in the present moment. The back of the chakra holds the energy of the situation. Another way to understand this is to picture the front of the chakra as "feeling" the emotions during a situation, and the back of the chakra as the "expression" of the energy or the "behavior" of the emotion. The front of the chakra describes the "feeling" and the back of the chakra describes the "action" of the chakra.

Once you've identified where the potential imbalances are in the energy body, the tables provide you tools to assist you in balancing the chakras. Each of the 7 Primary Chakras is associated with different attributes. Each chakra has a slightly different energy vibration.

Colors exist on a frequency of vibration. In Pranic healing, color visualization is used during the healing technique. One can imagine the color of the chakra combined with a bright white light. Sound vibrations can also affect the chakras. Each chakra has a different keynote and the sound vibrations from our vocal cord can open the chakras. Tools such as sound bowls can resonate at specific keynotes which open and release chakras allowing a deep meditative experience.

Essential oils can also be used to open the energy centers. Essential oils, combined with different breathing techniques, open and refresh the chakra system. Crystals radiate frequencies. Crystals open and stimulate chakras for health and healing.

Affirmations are powerful positive thoughts. Repeating an affirmation opens a chakra. Affirmations change one's perspective and outlook in life. Affirmations assist in manifesting our goals and encouraging us to keep moving forward.

These chakra charts are considered a companion guide to the book the **100 Chakra System, An Introduction to Negative Energy Release Work**. Raven introduces the concept that humans have 100 chakras, and advanced souls have up to 500 chakras. In this book, Raven gives a detailed explanation of the 7 Primary Chakras, the Higher Chakras, and the

Ascending Chakras. She examines the similarities and differences in the energy body and Lightbody. She discusses the anatomy of the energy body and Lightbody, and touches on developing your psychic skills to work more directly with your angelic team. This book also contains a self healing section to assist you in beginning your personal energy clearing practice.

These chakra charts are pulled from Part 2 of the 100 Chakra System and are presented in compact style for easier access as you start working to heal yourself and others. The chakra charts can also be used as pendulum charts to assist energy healing students in understanding where the blocks are, or how they should focus their healing sessions when working with clients.

For more information on how to use the divination tool of the pendulum with these charts, please refer to the book, the **3 Pendulum Languages**. In this book, Raven explains how you can use the pendulum to start communicating with your white light angelic team. The chakra charts are displayed in a circular fashion so you can place the pendulum at the center. You can then ask questions and watch for the swing to a word, feeling, or behavior. This book gives examples of how to have conversations with your angelic team. You can ask your team questions and then hold the pendulum over the charts to get the answers you seek. More information on how to use the pendulum to clear chakras will be presented in the upcoming book, **Chakra Balancing using the Pendulum**.

I hope you will join me in learning more about the 100 Chakra System and how you can use energy healing and meditation to clear and balance your chakras. The 7 Primary Chakras are the foundation chakras and are rooted in our present moment consciousness. Whatever is happening right here and right now, in your experience is reflected in the chakras of the energy body. As you move forward and advance your consciousness and understanding of the 100 chakras, it is vitally important to understand and memorize the themes and emotional attitudes of the 7 Primary Chakra. The healing work is rooted in your physical body and in our present moment.

To receive a free energy healing self-study course on how you can clear your chakras, please visit www.ravenlightbody.com.

Names of the 7 Primary Chakras

NUMBER	LOCATION	THEME	SANSKRIT
7	CROWN	CONNECTION	SAHASRARA
6	THIRD EYE	MIND	AJNA
5	THROAT	COMMUNICATION	VISHUDDHA
4	HEART	LOVE	ANAHATA
3	SOLAR PLEXUS	POWER	MUNIPURA
2	SACRAL	CREATIVE ENERGY	SVADHISTHANA
1	ROOT	GROUNDING	MULADHARA

LISTED BELOW ARE CRYSTALS THAT ONE CAN PLACE ON THE CHAKRA TO STIMULATE AND BALANCE. THIS IS A SHORT LIST FOR BEGINNERS TO GET STARTED.

	Name	Location	Theme	Crystals
1 chakra	Mūlādhāra मूलाधार	Root	Grounding	Agate, Amber, Ametrine, Bloodstone, Quartz, Jasper
2 chakra	Svadhishthana स्वाधिष्ठान	Sacral	Creative energy	Aquamarine, Danburite, Lepidolite, Serpentine, Sodalite
3 chakra	Manipūra मणिपूर	Solar plexus	Power	Beryl, Citrine, Cuprite, Lodestone, Pyrite, Smoky Quarts, Citrine, Labradorite
4 chakra	Anāhata अनाहत	Heart	Love	Amethyst, Aventurine, Azurite, Cuprite, Danburite, Diamond, Onyx
5 chakra	Viśuddha विशुद्ध	Throat	Communication	Angelite, Aquamarine, Blue Lace Agate, Kyanite, Lapis Lazuli
6 chakra	Ājñā आज्ञा	Third eye	Mind	Apophyllite, Malachite, Chrysoberyl, Chrysocolla, Obsidian, Herkimer Diamond, Sugillite
7 chakra	Sahasrāra सहस्रार	Crown	Connection	Aragonite, Celestine, Hematite, Lolite, Sapphire Selenite

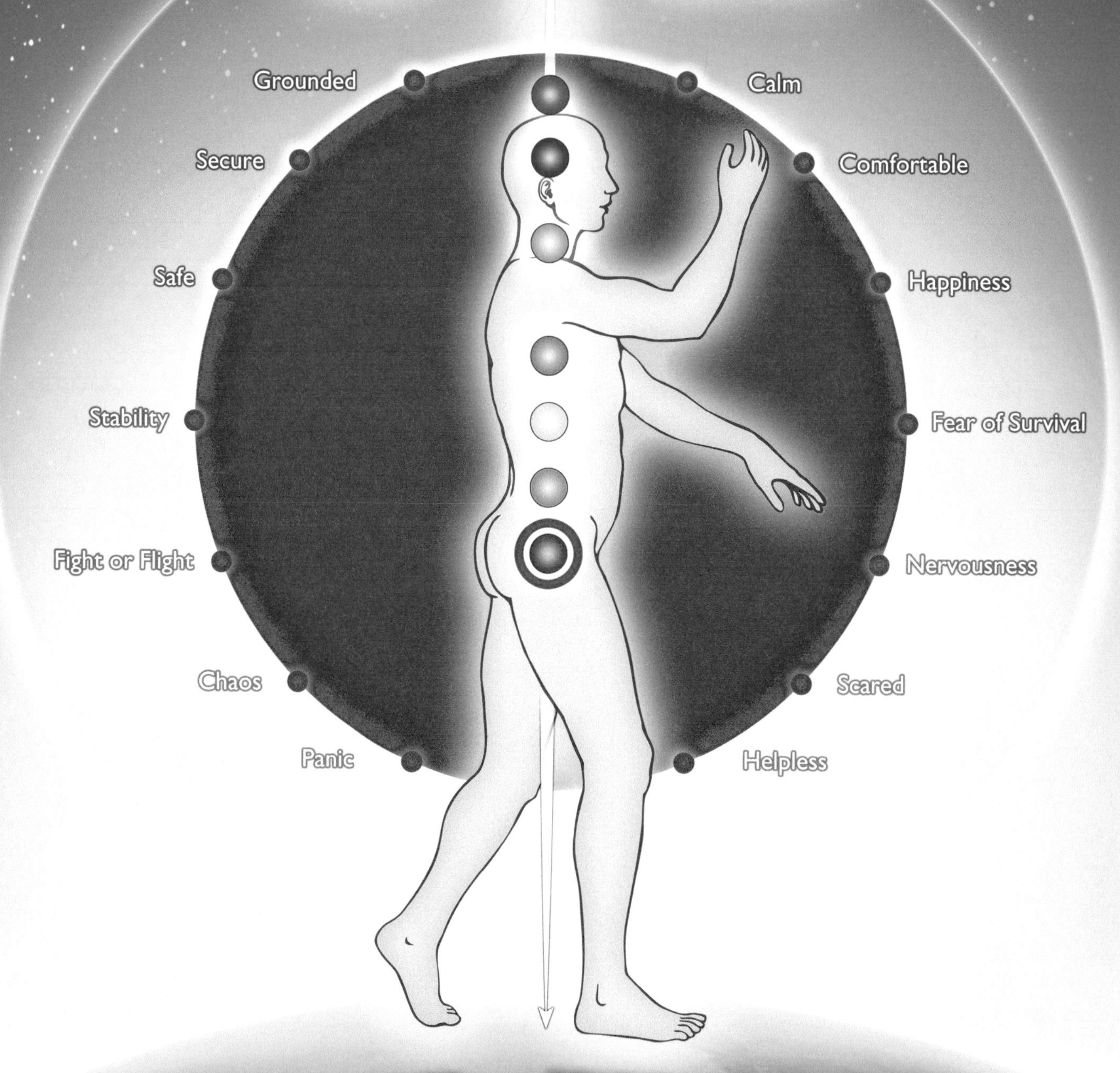
CHAKRA 1
Root, Muladhara, Grounding
ENERGY
EMOTIONS
Grounded
Secure
Safe
Stability
Fight or Flight
Chaos
Panic
Calm
Comfortable
Happiness
Fear of Survival
Nervousness
Scared
Helpless
SAFETY
GROUNDED
FOUNDATION
SURVIVAL

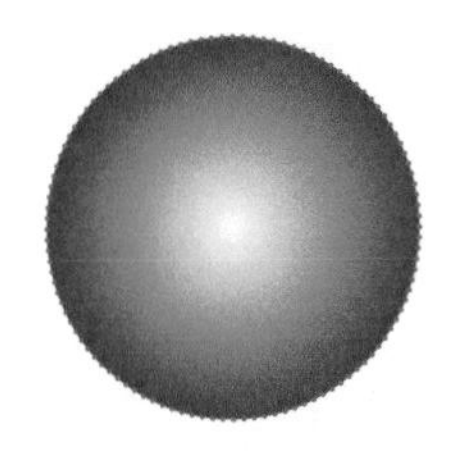

Chakra 1

Root Chakra,
Mūlādhāra मूलाधार
Grounding

ATTRIBUTES	
Location	Bottom of the Spine
Descriptive Words	Safety, Grounded, Foundation, Survival
Color	RED
Direction	Energy moving downward for grounding, energy moving up from the Earth
Seed Syllable	LAM
Keynote	C
Essential Oils	Cedarwood, Douglas Fir, Roman, Chamomile, Helichrysum, Rosemary
Crystals	Jasper, Agate, Bloodstone, Carnelian, Pyrite, Ruby

IN BALANCE	OUT OF BALANCE
Grounded	Stressed Out
Calm	Restlessness
Nature	Concrete Landscape
Safety	State of Emergency
Positive Change	Afraid of Change
Foundation	Earthquake
Survival	Lost or Homeless
Security	Feeling Threatened

Grounding Affirmations:

GROUNDING

I am safe, I am grounded.

I am grounded and rooted into the Earth.

I root down and feel connected,
I release restless energy.

I anchor to a solid foundation.

I am calm, I am poised.

I connect with nature.

SAFETY

I am safe, I am sound.

I am safe, I am completely safe.

In the mist of great change,
I ground down and feel safe.

It's only change,
I move through the transition feeling safe.

SURVIVAL

Everything I need comes me
exactly when I need it.

I always have plenty to eat and drink.

I call upon my angels
for protection and support.

Angels surround me, I am safe.

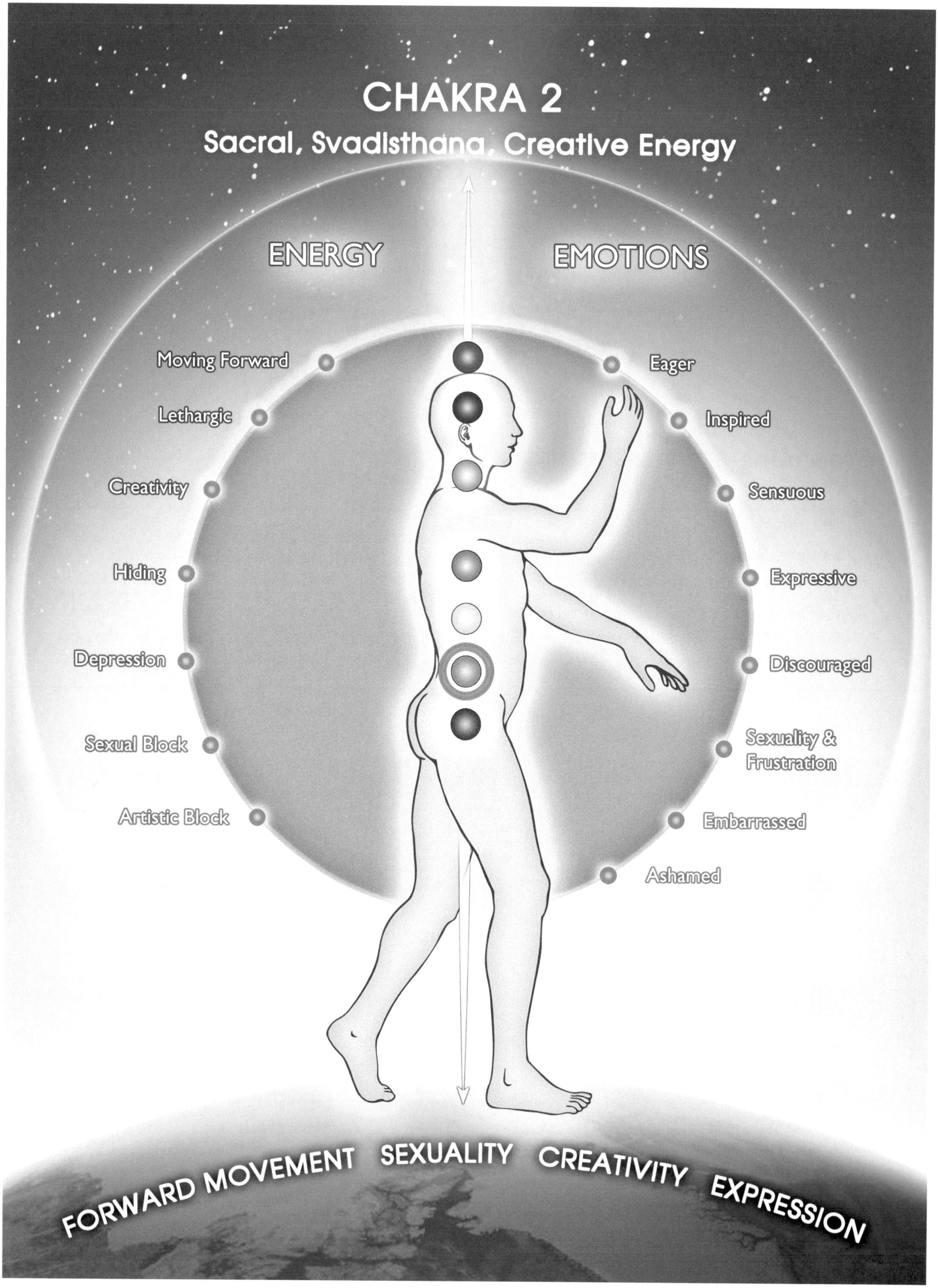

CHAKRA 2

Sacral, Svadisthana, Creative Energy

ENERGY

Moving Forward
Lethargic
Creativity
Hiding
Depression
Sexual Block
Artistic Block

EMOTIONS

Eager
Inspired
Sensuous
Expressive
Discouraged
Sexuality & Frustration
Embarrassed
Ashamed

FORWARD MOVEMENT SEXUALITY CREATIVITY EXPRESSION

Chakra 2

Sacral

Svadhishthana

स्वाधिष्ठान

Creative Energy

ATTRIBUTES	
Location	Below the Navel
Descriptive Words	Forward Movement, Sexuality, Creativity, Expression
Color	Orange
Direction	Chakra spins front and back
Seed Syllable	VAM
Keynote	D
Also Called	Navel
Essential Oils	Cardamon, Clary Sage, Cypress, Ylang Ylang, Jasmine
Crystals	Aquamarine, Danburite, Lepidolite, Serpentine, Sodalite

Creative Energy Affirmations:

MOVING FORWARD

I now move forward in my life.

I move in the direction of my greatest good.

I create an adventurous and amazing life.

I manifest by taking bold action steps.

I free myself, I am free.

I am motivated in the directions of my next potential.

I complete one baby step at a time.

SEXUALITY

I am free to be a sexual being.

I accept my sexuality, I am free.

CREATIVITY

I express myself artistically, I am free to create.

I birth new ideas into existence.

I create something unique in the world.

I have unlimited potential.

IN BALANCE	OUT OF BALANCE
Motivated	Feeling Stuck, Unmotivated
Drive	Unmotivated
Adventurous	Boredom
Focus on Tasks	Easily Distracted
Freedom	Life is Limited
Sexually Satisfied	Sexual Block
Sexual Acceptance	Sexual Block
Creativity	Lacking Artistic Expression
Procreation	No Birth or Outcome
Unique Expression	No Expression
Potential	Limited

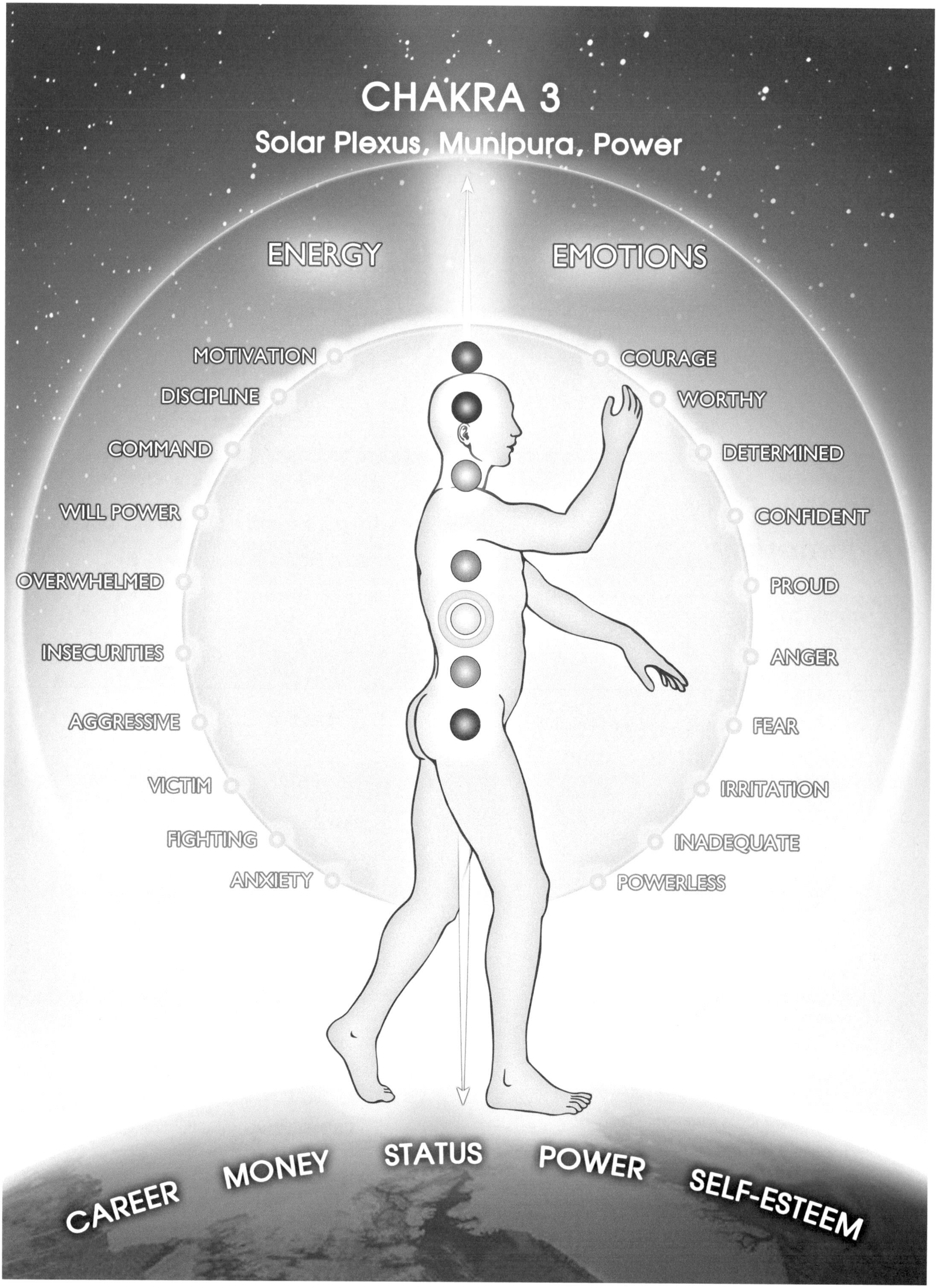

CHAKRA 3

Solar Plexus, Munipura, Power

ENERGY

MOTIVATION
DISCIPLINE
COMMAND
WILL POWER
OVERWHELMED
INSECURITIES
AGGRESSIVE
VICTIM
FIGHTING
ANXIETY

EMOTIONS

COURAGE
WORTHY
DETERMINED
CONFIDENT
PROUD
ANGER
FEAR
IRRITATION
INADEQUATE
POWERLESS

CAREER MONEY STATUS POWER SELF-ESTEEM

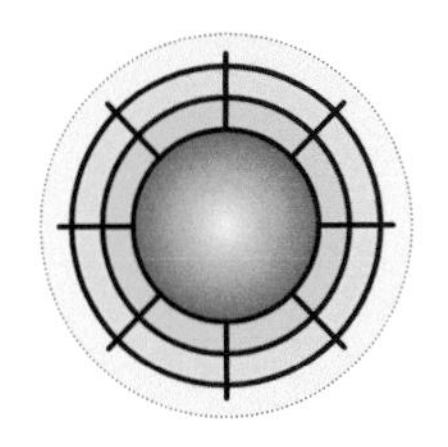

Chakra 3

Solar Plexus

Manipūra मणिपूर

Power

ATTRIBUTES	
Location	Above the Belly Bottom
Descriptive Words	Power, Self-Esteem, Courage, Money, Status
Color	Yellow
Direction	Front and Back
Seed Syllable	RAM
Keynote	E
Also Called	Core
Essential Oils	Bergamot, Cardamon, Clove, Geranium, Helichrysum, Lemon, Myrrh, Wild Orange
Crystals	Beryl, Citrine, Cuprite, Lodestone, Pyrite, Smoky Quarts, Labradorite

IN BALANCE	OUT OF BALANCE
Self-Confidence	Low Self Esteem
Self-Discipline	Easily Gives In
Self-Esteem	Insecurities
Self Advocacy	Pushed Down or Held Back
Balanced Power	Dominating/Powerless
Will-Power	Weakness
Strength	Anger Towards Others
Courageous	Fearful or Timid
Fair Leadership	Dominating/Powerless
Career Stability	Fear of Career Loss
Controlled Stance	Fierce and Unyielding
Balanced Response	Anger at Community

Power Affirmations:

RIGHT POWER – SELF GOVERNING

I communicate with strong loving words.

I am confident in my abilities to succeed.

I am worthy and I am confident.

I am disciplined, I stay focused.

I am committed
and follow through with tasks.

With great courage I accomplish my goals.

I stand up and lovingly assert my truth.

Within me lies the energy
to accomplish all I will to do

EXPRESSION WITH OTHERS

I am strong, I am courageous.

I am worthy of love and respect.

I harmonize and respect others.

I balance my power
and consider all involved.

I lead with balanced power.

I am willing to listen.

CAREER OR MONEY

I am guided to make changes in my career,

I promote myself.

I move in the direction of my greatest good and highest happiness.

The perfect new job comes in
to provide what I need.

Money is coming to me quickly and easily.

I exude confidence.

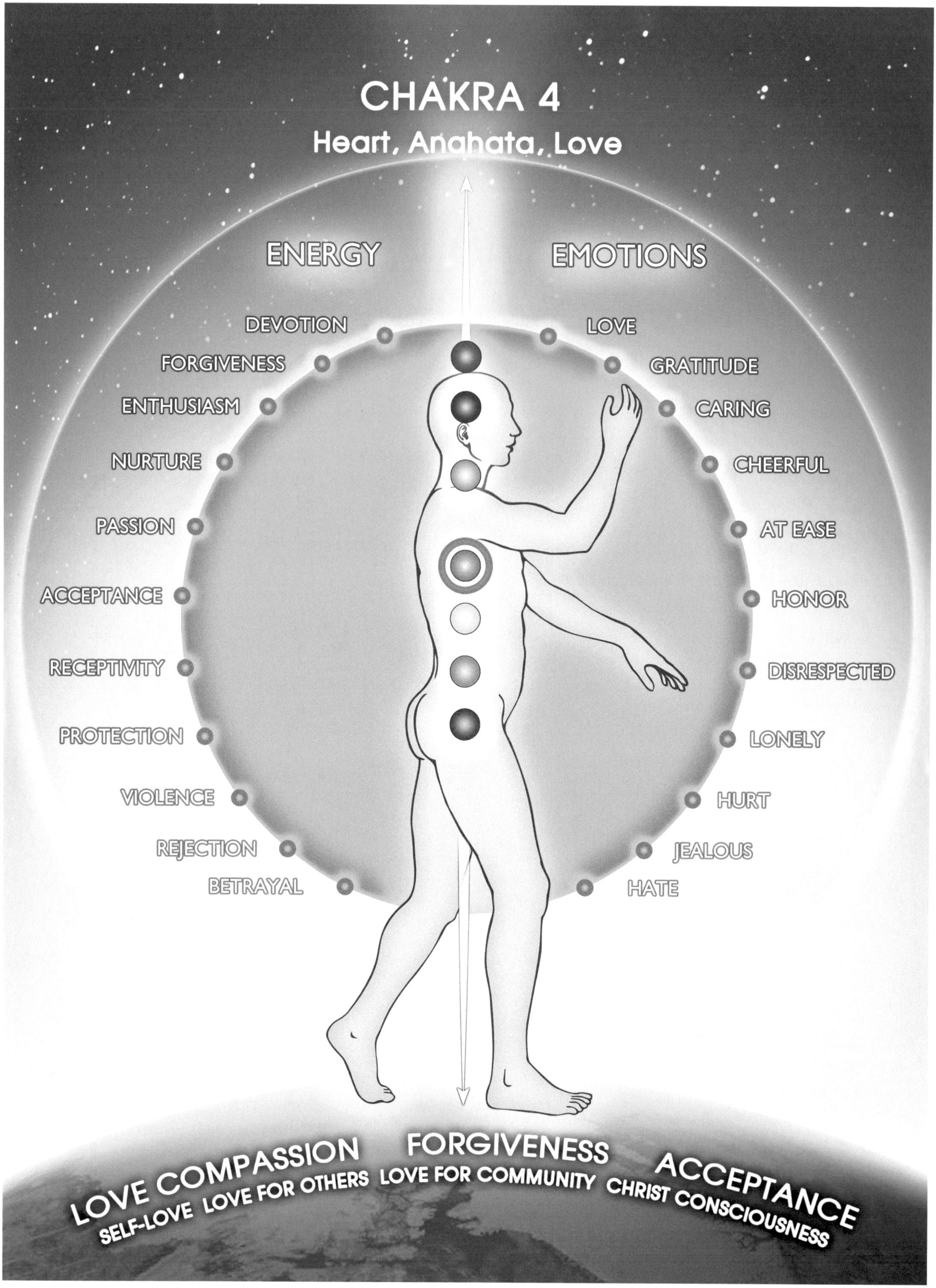

CHAKRA 4

Heart, Anahata, Love

ENERGY

DEVOTION
FORGIVENESS
ENTHUSIASM
NURTURE
PASSION
ACCEPTANCE
RECEPTIVITY
PROTECTION
VIOLENCE
REJECTION
BETRAYAL

EMOTIONS

LOVE
GRATITUDE
CARING
CHEERFUL
AT EASE
HONOR
DISRESPECTED
LONELY
HURT
JEALOUS
HATE

LOVE COMPASSION FORGIVENESS ACCEPTANCE

SELF-LOVE LOVE FOR OTHERS LOVE FOR COMMUNITY CHRIST CONSCIOUSNESS

Chakra 4

Heart

Anāhata अनाहत

Love

Love Affirmations:

LOVE YOURSELF

I love myself, I deserve the very best.
I am love, loving and beloved.
I am worthy, I am loveable.
I am unique and special.
I love and appreciate myself.
I love and accept myself.
I am beautiful, I appreciate my form.

LOVE FOR INTIMATE LOVERS & FAMILY

I am open to giving and receiving love.
I forgive myself for contributing to hurt feelings.
I forgive you for hurting my feelings.
I forgive everyone involved in the situation.
I am compassionate and willing to forgive.
I soften my heart, I am gentle.
I exchange hateful feelings for love.
I connect from my heart to your heart.
I accept my family as they are and create appropriate boundaries.
I accept what I cannot change, I heal my heart.
I accept things as they are, not how I would like them to be, in this acceptance, I am free.

LOVE FOR COMMUNITY

I am open to other points of view.
I open to universal love and share it with all.
I remember everyone has a touch of light, even those shrouded in darkness.
I hold compassion for others that are having a tough day.
I am brave and meet new friends that share my interest.
I remember not everyone is aligned to the light, I send them love.
I am open and accept others.

LOVE FOR DIVINE SOURCE

I connect and receive from my Higherself
I connect and receive from all that is
I experience joy in my everyday
I channel in love, light and joy
To all beings everywhere, love and compassion
Om Shanti, Peace

ATTRIBUTES	
Location	Heart
Descriptive Words	Love, Compassion, Forgiveness, Acceptance
Color	Green
Direction	Chakra spins front and back
Seed Syllable	YAM
Keynote	F
Also Called	Core
Essential Oils	Frankincense, Lavendar, Patchouli, Roman Chamolie, Wild Orange, Ylang Ylang, Rosemary, Sandalwood, Rose, Angelic Root
Crystals	Amazonite, Amethyst, Angelite, Azurite, Green Calcite, Diamond, Opal, Rose Quartz

IN BALANCE	OUT OF BALANCE	
Self-Love	Feel Unworthy of Love	SELF
Self-Love	Feels Unlovable	SELF
Self-Acceptance	Feels Ugly or Defective	SELF
Compassion for Self	Despise Oneself	SELF
Giving and Receiving	Gives to Depletion	Significant Others
Willing to Forgive	Holding a Grudge	Significant Others
Loving and Caring	Anger and Mean	Significant Others
Emotional Connection	Disconnected in Relationship	Significant Others
Compassion for Family	Distain of Family	Significant Others
Compassion for All	Hatred towards Some	Community
Love for Community	Feels Disrespected	Community
Social Friendships	Isolation and Withdrawal	Community
Accepting of Others	Judgmental	Community
Divine Connection	Hurt by God	Divinity
Love to all Being Everywhere	Considers only the Self	Divinity

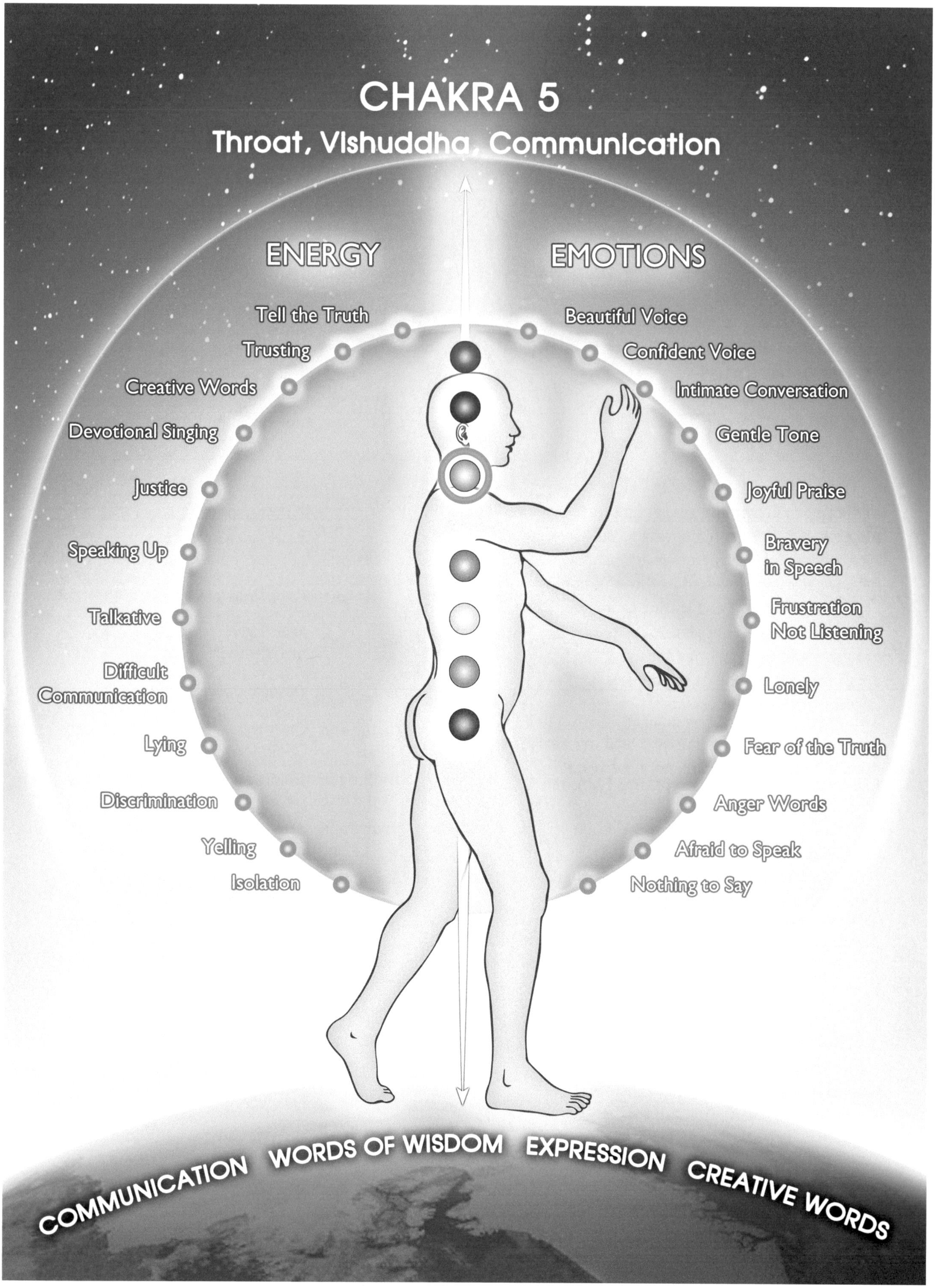

CHAKRA 5

Throat, Vishuddha, Communication

ENERGY

Tell the Truth
Trusting
Creative Words
Devotional Singing
Justice
Speaking Up
Talkative
Difficult Communication
Lying
Discrimination
Yelling
Isolation

EMOTIONS

Beautiful Voice
Confident Voice
Intimate Conversation
Gentle Tone
Joyful Praise
Bravery in Speech
Frustration Not Listening
Lonely
Fear of the Truth
Anger Words
Afraid to Speak
Nothing to Say

COMMUNICATION WORDS OF WISDOM EXPRESSION CREATIVE WORDS

Chakra 5
Throat
Viśuddha वशिुद्ध
Communication

ATTRIBUTES	
Location	Throat
Descriptive Words	Communication, Words of Wisdom, Expression, Creative Words
Color	Sky Blue
Direction	Chakra spins front and back
Seed Syllable	HAM
Keynote	G
Essential Oils	Cinnamon Bark, Cypress, Lavender, Patchouli, Peppermint, Vetiver, Ylang Ylang
Crystals	Angelite, Aquamarine, Blue Lace Agate, Kyanite, Lapis Lazuli

Communication Affirmations:

COMUNICATION

I am willing to listen.
I communication with strong loving words.
I courageously speak up.
I speak positive words and uplifting words.
I speak with beautiful vibration in my voice.
I speak my truth.
I stand up for my truth.

EXPRESSION

I express my true self.
I am willing to express myself
I am upfront and honest.
I speak with words of confidence.
I speak with a gentle voice.
I hum a happy tune.
I artistically express myself.
I express my inner voice.

WORDS OF WISDOM

I think before I speak.
I think before I ask a difficult question.
I tune into my Higherself and respond with wisdom.

IN BALANCE	OUT OF BALANCE
Listening	Speaking and Not Being Heard
Communication Received	Frustrated with Communication
Strong Social Exchange	Afraid to Speak in Groups
Speaking One's Truth	Afraid to Speak
Stand up for Boundaries	Afraid to Assert Oneself
Positive Speech	Negative Words, Cursing
Beautiful Vibration in the Voice	Complaining and Whining Voice
Gentle Words	Angry or Nagging Voice
Open and Upfront	Hiding
Word of Confidence	Mumbling, Timid Voice
Self Expression	Suppressed, Not Spoken
Creativity in Vocal Expression	No Singing, Writing, Poetry, Drama
Meaningful Communication	Words are Meaningless
Thoughtful Words	Speaking Without Consideration

CHAKRA 6

Third Eye, Ajna, Mind

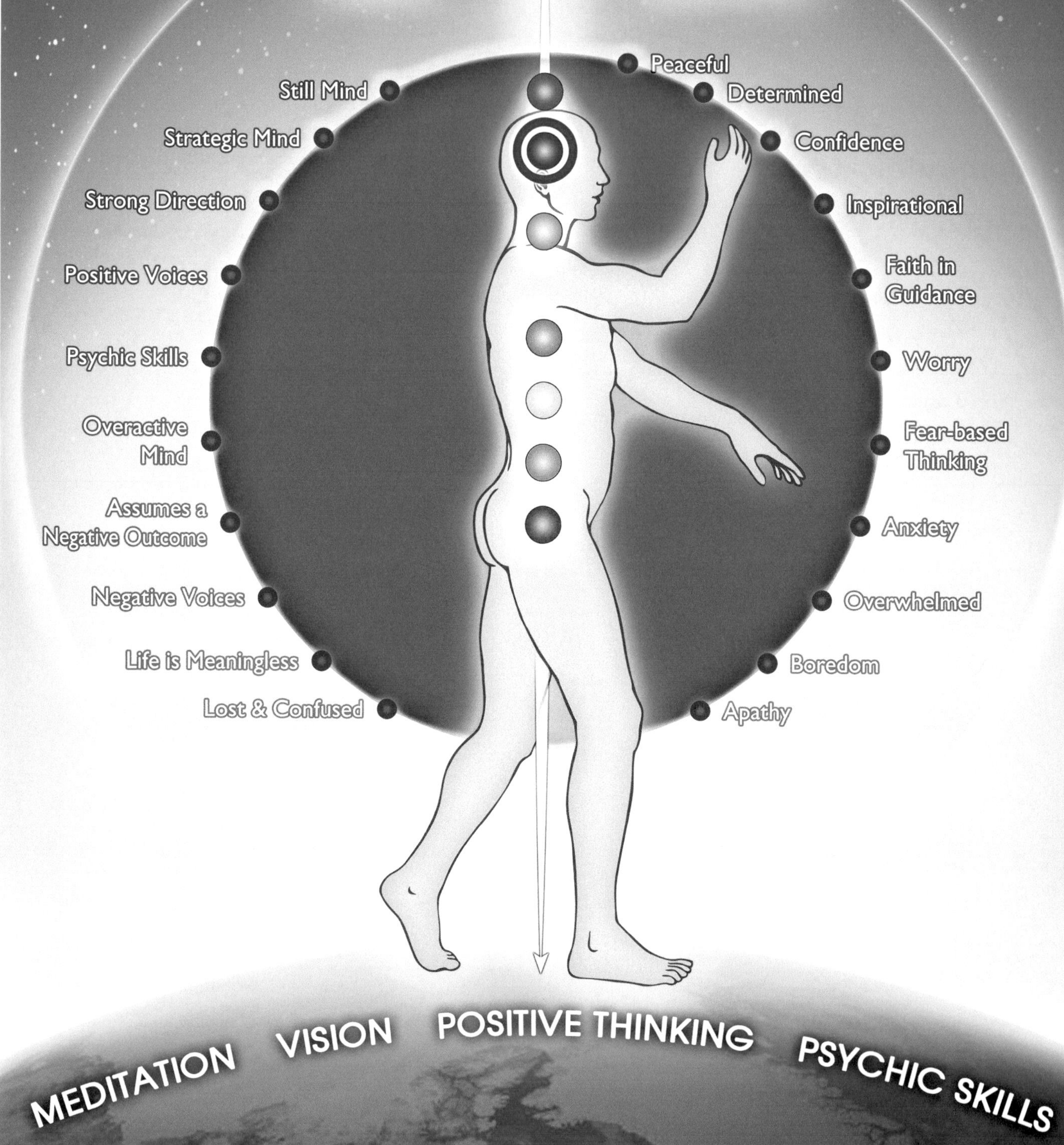

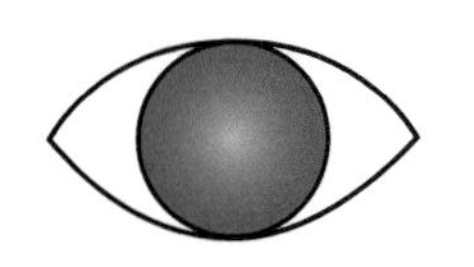

Chakra 6
Third Eye
Ājñā आज्ञा
Mind

ATTRIBUTES	
Location	Forehead
Descriptive Words	Meditation, Vision, Positive Thinking, Psychic Awareness
Color	Indigo
Direction	Chakra spins front and back at a Diagonal Angle
Seed Syllable	AUM
Keynote	A
Essential Oils	Clary Sage, Peppermint, Sandalwood, Vetiver, Ylang Ylang, Frankincense, Juniper, Angelic Root
Crystals	Apophyllite, Malachite, Chrysoberyl, Chrysocolla, Obsidian, Herkimer Diamond, Sugillite

IN BALANCE	OUT OF BALANCE
Clear Direction	Unclear Direction, Undecided
Strong Decision Making	Unable to Make a Decision
Walking on Life Path	Off Path
Learn or Teach Knowledge	Not Challenged Intellectually
Believe in Yourself	Doubt Yourself
Positive Thinking	Negative Thinking
Focused Intentions	Doesn't Complete Tasks
Affirmations	Negative Attitude
Disciplined Mind	Overthinking
Positive Voices	Negative Voices
Focused Mind	Undisciplined Mind
Present Moment Consciousness	Distracted
Meditation	No Concept of Meditation
Quiet the Mind	Overactive Mind

Mind Affirmations:

MEDITATIVE MIND

I stay present in the moment, I am here now.
I quite my thoughts, I quite my mind.
I relax my mind and open to my Higherself.
I focus my mind on the breath.
I open my third eye to higher levels of consciousness.
I am focus and quiet my mind.

VISION

My vision is clear, I take bold action steps.
I search and grow until my vision is clear.
I visualize my success.
I take a bold leap of faith. I achieve my goals.
I believe in myself.

THINKING MIND

I train my mind to slow down and quiet.
I train my mind to think positively.
I am flexible and adaptable when there is change.
I focused and complete my tasks.
I am calm, peaceful, tranquil, relaxed.
My mind is am instrument for my Higherself.

POSTIVE THINKING

I am also safe, I am protected and everything goes my way.

Everything I need comes to me, exactly when I need it.

Resources are coming to me quickly and easily.

PSYCHIC SKILLS

I open inner doorways to higher dimensions.
I activate my third eye and awaken my spiritual gifts.

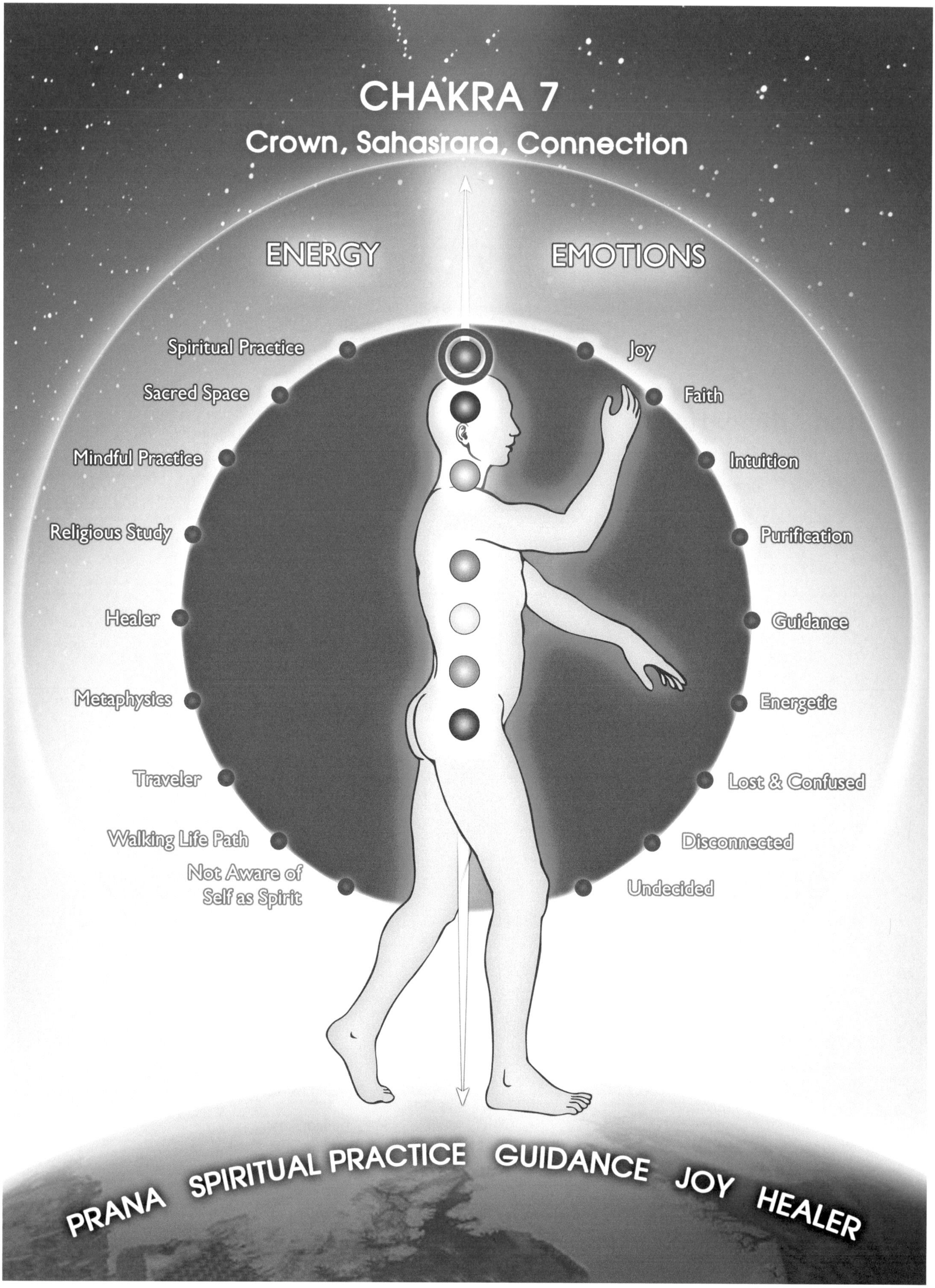

CHAKRA 7

Crown, Sahasrara, Connection

ENERGY

Spiritual Practice
Sacred Space
Mindful Practice
Religious Study
Healer
Metaphysics
Traveler
Walking Life Path
Not Aware of Self as Spirit

EMOTIONS

Joy
Faith
Intuition
Purification
Guidance
Energetic
Lost & Confused
Disconnected
Undecided

PRANA SPIRITUAL PRACTICE GUIDANCE JOY HEALER

Chakra 7

Crown

Sahasrāra सहस्रार

Connection

ATTRIBUTES	
Location	Crown of the Head
Descriptive Words	Prana, Spiritual Practice, Connection, Guidance, Joy
Color	Purple
Direction	Chakra direction is upward
Seed Syllable	AUM
Keynote	B
Essential Oils	Arborvitae, Frankincense, Lavender, Myrrh, Vetiver, Spikenard
Crystals	Aragonite, Celestine, Hematite, Lolite, Sapphire, Selenite

Connection Affirmations:

CONNECTION

I AM LOVE.

I AM THAT.

I am open and receiving love from God.

I open to the infinite and feel peace.

I am overflowing with energy,
I have enough to give to others.

I am a multi-dimensional being.

I connect to the light.

I remember who I am.

JOY

I AM JOY!

Energy and joy comes into my body,
I fill up with JOY! I am enthusiastic!

GUIDANCE

I follow my intuition.

I listen to my guidance system.

I know what is right and wrong for me.

I go to spiritual practice,
it feeds my soul.

I know when to take time for myself.

I am a uniquely gifted spiritual being.

IN BALANCE	OUT OF BALANCE
Connection to Divine Source	Disconnected from Universal Love
Relationship with Higher Power	Aware of God, But not in Relationship
Self-Defined or Religious Path	No Spiritual Practice
Joyful Expression	Inner Sorrow
Pranic Healer	Unconscious of the Light
Highly Intuitive	Negative Outcomes
Guidance	No Discernment of Right or Wrong Path
Solitude	No DownTime
Multi-Dimensional	Limited Consciousness

Higher Chakras 8-15

ASCENDING CHAKRAS 2D
Chakra Clusters Diagram of Energy Patterns

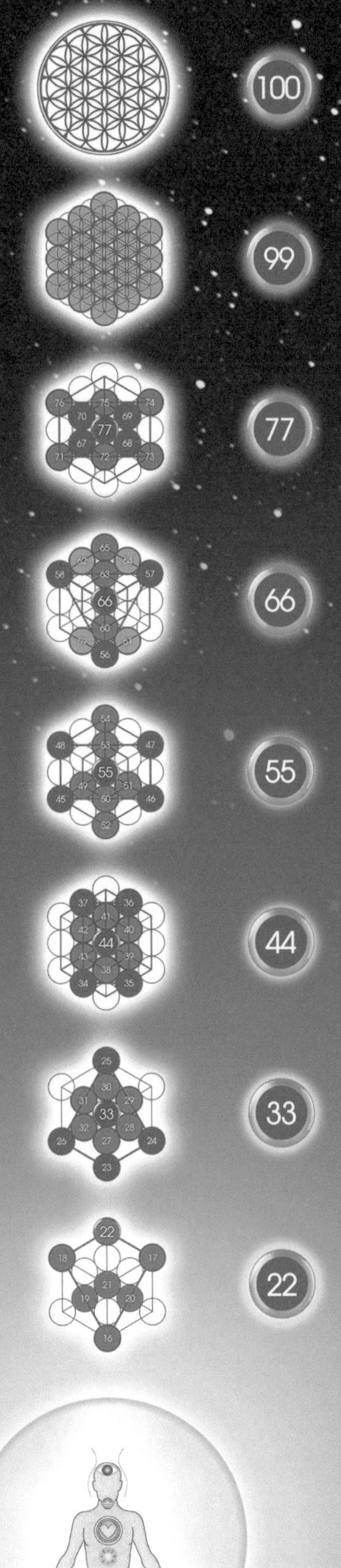

Clear to the 100th Chakra

Ascending Chakras

Higher Chakras

7 Primary Chakras

Printed in the United States
By Bookmasters